What was it like Before the Telephone?

Paul Humphrey

Illustrated by
Lynda Stevens

Evans

We're visiting the science museum.

4

This is the communications room. It has lots of pictures and other things that tell us how people sent messages before the telephone was invented.

6

How did people send messages using all these funny things?

Come with me and you'll find out.

7

How do you think people sent messages to each other before telephones?

That's right. This picture shows a mail carrier. Hundreds of years ago, he carried letters and parcels to people across Britain and Europe.

I bet it took him ages to deliver each letter.

9

But people sent messages even before that. They used drums to beat out the message.

Some of the Indian tribes of North America used fire to communicate. They sent smoke signals.

I wonder what they are saying?

Look at the funny towers on this model.

Those are semaphore towers. People could send messages from one hilltop to another by raising or lowering the arms.

Other people sent
semaphore messages using flags.

But what happened if it was foggy?

*No one could
see the message.*

13

That is a carrier pigeon. People would put messages into that little container on its leg. Then they would send it flying to the person receiving the message.

People wanted to send more complicated messages, so they made pens out of feathers. They sharpened the end and dipped it in ink and wrote their message.

A postal system was set up and letters and parcels were carried by stagecoach from one person to another.

In America, Pony Express riders galloped thousands of kilometres from one side of the country to the other.

I would like to have been a Pony Express rider!

It's a lantern for flashing out a message in code. It is called the Morse Code.

A long flash is called a dash and a short flash is called a dot. Does anyone know any Morse Code?

I do, ···−−−··· means S.O.S or Help!

23

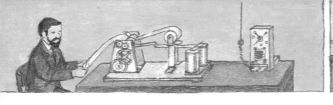

Of course, you had to be able to see the flashes of light to get the message. The next invention used electricity to send the Morse Code message along wires.

The telegraph operator would tap out a message on a transmitter like this one. But you still had to be able to read the code.

The next invention was a big step forward. It meant that messages could be sent over long distances and that people could talk just normally. What was it?

The telephone!

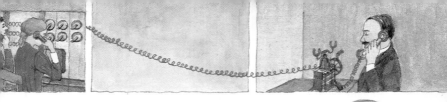

But what's this funny looking thing?

That is what a very
early telephone looked like.

People have always wanted to send messages to each other. Today we can use the telephone to talk to people all over the world. We can even send a written message instantly using a fax machine.

We've come a long way from smoke signals and carrier pigeons!

29

Can you remember how each of the things on this page were used to send messages?

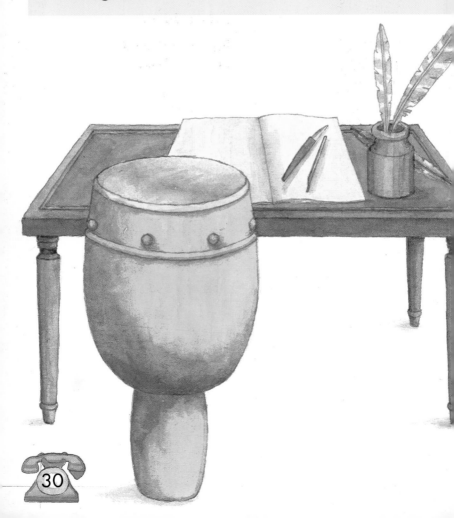